I want young Americans to see

how someone lived in the twentieth century and how this person could collect works of art the way I have.... I want to share this with the rest of the world. Maybe it'll be an incentive to some people. Maybe it won't, but at least they'll get a chance to see how I lived.

———————————————————

Marjorie Merriweather Post

WITH CONTRIBUTIONS BY
Kate Markert
Lynn Rossotti
Liana Paredes

WASHINGTON, D.C.

CONTENTS

7 *Foreword*

8 *Estate*
Marjorie Merriweather Post
Hillwood: Marjorie Merriweather Post's Living Legacy

52 *Museum*
Collecting with Passion, Connoisseurship, and Style

86 *Gardens*
A Country Estate in the Nation's Capital

112 *Selected Resources*

FOREWORD

Welcome to the oasis that Marjorie Merriweather Post created at Hillwood Estate, Museum & Gardens. As the sole heir to the Postum Cereal Company (later known as General Foods), Marjorie stood out among the wealthiest women of her time. She was also one of the era's most progressive figures, exerting a strong hand in the business affairs of her company long before women appeared in the board rooms of major corporations. In addition to her business acumen, Marjorie directed her intense focus on collecting French eighteenth- and nineteenth-century decorative arts and Russian imperial art, as well as on making significant charitable contributions throughout her adult life.

Hillwood remains her most important legacy. Here, in her home surrounded by twenty-five acres of manicured gardens and woodlands bordering on Rock Creek Park, she crafted a spectacular repository for her museum-quality collections. She then made the estate and the mansion with its magnificent holdings a gift to the nation and to the world, leaving them for everyone to enjoy as she had. Through her generosity and foresight, we can all marvel at the intricate beauty of the Fabergé Easter eggs, stroll the paths in the rose garden, and admire the expansive view of the Lunar Lawn. We can imagine being received in the French drawing room, dining on Sèvres porcelain, and watching movies in the pavilion as honored guests attending one of Marjorie's famous social evenings. The perfect unity that Marjorie created between the interior and exterior "rooms" of Hillwood, such as the wonderful views from her exquisite French-style bedroom out to the delicate French parterre and beyond, is now left for us to savor.

We hope this book provides memories of a wonderful visit to Hillwood and inspires you to come back for a closer look in another season or to see a special exhibition at this splendid haven in the nation's capital city.

KATE MARKERT
Executive Director

Hillwood Estate, Museum & Gardens opened to the public in 1977, fulfilling Marjorie Merriweather Post's wish to make her collection available for the enjoyment and edification of future generations. Her residence in the heart of Washington was conceived as both a home and a museum to showcase her collection of Russian and western European decorative arts.

PREVIOUS: South portico © Maxwell MacKenzie

OPPOSITE: Marjorie Merriweather Post in Marie Antoinette costume. Frame by Edward F. Caldwell and Company. New York, 1927

Marjorie Merriweather Post

On November 3, 1957, enveloped by the golden fall colors of her newly created garden oasis in Washington, D.C., and by the good cheer of friends made over her lifetime, Marjorie Merriweather Post was led to the gated entrance of a beautifully landscaped pathway. There, she encountered a plaque that still reads:

Friendship Walk—Hillwood
Dedicated by her friends
as a tribute to
Marjorie Merriweather Post
for her generous nature,
love of beauty and devotion
to human needs.

This garden path, affectionately called the Friendship Walk, was a gift planned in secret by a group of Marjorie's friends in honor of both her seventieth birthday and her remarkable philanthropic contributions. It remains a reminder that the creation of Hillwood itself was a culmination of Marjorie's life. The daughter of a self-made man, Marjorie was influenced by her father's pioneering spirit, industriousness, and practicality. She employed her innate drive, keen intellect, and generous spirit to become a businesswoman in her own right and a supporter of charitable causes. With exceptional aesthetic vision, this worldly art collector left Hillwood as her final and most lasting legacy.

ABOVE: Charles William (C.W.) Post and daughter, Marjorie, 1889. Courtesy Bentley Historical Library, University of Michigan

RIGHT: Marjorie's mother, Ella Merriweather Post, 1905

OPPOSITE: *Portrait of Marjorie Merriweather Post*, by Frank O. Salisbury. United States, 1934. Oil on canvas

ESTATE

Early advertising for Post Grape-Nuts

A SEAT AT THE BREAKFAST TABLE

Marjorie Merriweather Post was born in 1887 in Springfield, Illinois. She was the only child of Ella Merriweather (1853–1912) and the industrialist and inventor Charles William Post (1854–1914), who founded the Postum Cereal Company. C.W.'s road to success directly resulted from his quest for better health. He suffered from an unexplained illness throughout adulthood, and as a Christian Scientist, he sought relief through spiritual healing and nutrition. In keeping with these guiding principles, Post endeavored to create products that would help his fellow man. In 1895 he introduced Postum, a grain-based beverage that he considered to be healthier than coffee, tea, and other caffeine-based drinks.

C.W. had earlier stayed at the Battle Creek Sanitarium founded by Dr. John Harvey Kellogg in Michigan. That visit prompted his idea to create a better-tasting cold breakfast cereal. He soon produced Grape-Nuts, one of the first ready-to-eat cold cereals, and with it established the beginnings of a breakfast cereal empire. C.W. further applied his ingenuity to pioneer marketing and promotion strategies for his products. Using creative paid advertising, slogans, free samples, and recipe booklets, he developed innovative marketing tactics that are now considered industry standards. Over time C.W.'s small cereal company grew into a global enterprise: General Foods.

With his daughter as his only heir, C.W. fully initiated Marjorie into all facets of the family business. She was just seven years old when her father founded Postum. Over the years Marjorie absorbed the range of his talents and acquired an early understanding of the intricacies of business management. Building on C.W.'s success, Marjorie learned about automation and manufacturing efficiency during factory visits and was introduced to the proceedings of board meetings. Decades later, after serving on the board of General Foods for twenty-two years, Marjorie wrote to the board's chairman with a suggestion for an advertising strategy for the multibillion-dollar business that grew from her father's quest for a healthy breakfast cereal.

As we approached Battle Creek on the train I was of course glued to the window, and I find that there still is no way of identifying what our factories are.... We pay millions of dollars a year for advertising General Foods, and here is a good chance to get free advertising, and for years we have not been availing ourselves of the opportunity.[1]

Board of Postum Cereal Company meeting in Battle Creek, Michigan, 1910s

ABOVE: Marjorie on her graduation from Mount Vernon Seminary in Washington, D.C., 1904

RIGHT: Wedding portrait of Marjorie and Edward Bennett Close, 1905

STEPPING INTO SOCIETY

The overwhelming success of Postum Cereal Company created a new outlook for C.W. Post, and he naturally wanted to share his achievements with his only child, but having Marjorie lead the family business was not a realistic goal at the turn of the twentieth century. Instead, C.W. sought to broaden his daughter's horizons with a worldly education.

In 1901, at the age of fourteen, Marjorie left the Midwest and enrolled in Mount Vernon Seminary in Washington, D.C. At this exclusive finishing school, she was introduced to East Coast high society and received her first official education in European and American history, art history, and music. Upon her graduation three years later, C.W. took his daughter overseas, where he rented a coach-and-four to show her the countryside of southern England and its stately homes, including Windsor Castle and Bushey Hall. By the time she returned to the United States, Marjorie

was prepared to enter the East Coast aristocracy by marrying one of its members. In 1905 she wed Edward Bennett Close, a law student from a prominent family in Greenwich, Connecticut.

C.W. built a house in Greenwich for the young couple. Marjorie experimented with interior decoration, and together she and her father chose furnishings rooted in the late Victorian era that mirrored his preferences. After the birth of her first two children—Adelaide in July 1908 and Eleanor eighteen months later—Marjorie sought to stimulate her mind by taking art and architecture courses at a nearby private school. From this early exposure Marjorie began to acquire her own taste for beautiful things, a characteristic that became more focused in later decades.

Marjorie's life took a dramatic turn when her mother died in 1912. Less than two years later, C.W.'s lifelong struggle with poor health led to depression and ultimately death. At the age of twenty-eight, Marjorie became the owner of the Postum Cereal Company, then worth $20 million, and one of the wealthiest women in the United States. The gender divide of the early twentieth century prevented her from officially running the company, but she made her opinions known through her husband, Ed Close, who joined the board upon C.W.'s death.

Portrait of Marjorie's daughters, Adelaide Brevoort Close and Eleanor Post Close, by Pierre Tartoué, 1910–19

Drawing room of the Burden Mansion, New York, ca. 1920

During the second decade of the twentieth century, Marjorie's interest in collecting was shaped and her commitment to charitable giving was solidified. Her fast-paced life included business and social commitments that often took her to New York City. The family initially rented and later purchased the Burden Mansion, a grand Beaux Arts structure located at the corner of Fifth Avenue and Ninety-second Street, for $10 million in 1916. Inspired by the palatial French interiors of the house, Marjorie surrounded herself with eighteenth-century furnishings suited to a woman of her status. She sought inspiration in the writings of novelist Edith Wharton and interior decorator Elsie de Wolfe, and she hired decorators to assist her in creating elegant interiors, particularly in the neoclassical style of Louis XVI, which was then in vogue among New York's fashionable society. Mitchell Samuels of French and Company, a decorating and antiques firm based in New York, helped Marjorie furnish the mansion's European period-style rooms.

One critical influence on the development of her collecting tastes was Sir Joseph Duveen. A British art dealer whose clients included business magnates and art collectors Henry Clay Frick, J.P. Morgan, Andrew Mellon, and John D. Rockefeller, Duveen introduced Marjorie to the arts and culture of eighteenth-century France. Although she avoided Duveen's enticements to acquire Old Master paintings, Marjorie established herself among the discerning collectors of European decorative art. She purchased two remarkable eighteenth-century Beauvais tapestries designed by François Boucher for her Louis XVI-style drawing room, as well as exquisite examples of eighteenth-century French furniture and Sèvres porcelains. The elements of harmony, balance, delicate decoration, and superb craftsmanship that defined these French objects guided Marjorie's collecting taste for the rest of her life.

Her charitable work at this period also shaped her lifetime of philanthropy. Like her father, Marjorie was a practicing Christian Scientist, and she allowed his early influence to direct her philosophy of giving.

HE WAS VERY CLEAR ON THE SUBJECT OF MONEY AND HOW IT CAN POSSESS PEOPLE AND TURN THEM INTO PERFECT FOOLS. HIS THEORY WAS THAT MONEY MUST BE KEPT WORKING AND IT MUST BE PRODUCTIVE. IT DOESN'T AMOUNT TO ANYTHING WHEN YOU HOARD IT, AND YOU'RE CRAMPING YOUR OWN MENTALITY IF YOU GET A MISERLY THOUGHT IN YOUR MIND....

SO, THAT TRAINING WITH ME HAS MEANT THAT I WANT TO KEEP IT WORKING, PRODUCING ONE THING AFTER ANOTHER, HELPING PEOPLE WHO ARE WORTHY AND WHO NEED IT, HELPING WITH EDUCATION, HELPING WITH CREATING BEAUTY.[2]

Her first endeavor began when she volunteered with the Red Cross following the entry of the United States into World War I. While she found donating her time was meaningful, she yearned to do more. On July 30, 1917, the SS *Saratoga* set sail from New York Harbor, carrying medical supplies worth approximately $75,000 that Marjorie had donated to establish an army hospital in Savenay, France. Unfortunately, the ship was accidentally sunk by the SS *Panama* en route to Europe. The crew survived, but the cargo did not. Marjorie provided a second round of supplies that arrived safely in France, and the Number 8 Base Hospital in Savenay became the largest Red Cross military medical facility of the era.[3]

FROZEN FOOD TO FABERGÉ

In 1919 Marjorie divorced Ed Close and married Wall Street financier Edward F. (E.F.) Hutton. Perfectly matched, the Huttons epitomized the carefree lifestyle of the Roaring Twenties. Marjorie hosted and attended a stream of events in both New York City and Palm Beach, Florida. Together the Huttons had one child, Nedenia, who as an actress took the name Dina Merrill.

With E.F. Hutton as chairman of the board, the Postum Cereal Company was transformed into the General Foods Corporation. It became a pioneer in frozen and prepared foods by acquiring Jell-O, Swans Down Cake Flour, Maxwell House Coffee, and Clarence Birdseye's burgeoning business in frozen foods. Burden Mansion remained the headquarters of Marjorie and E.F.'s professional and personal lives, but with the purchase of grand properties on Long Island, in the Adirondacks, and in Palm Beach, Marjorie could both advance her social station and develop her connoisseurship by adding to her important collection of furnishings and decorative art objects.

FAR LEFT: Marjorie and Edward Francis (E.F.) Hutton with their daughter Nedenia, ca. 1924

LEFT: Marjorie with an unknown child at the Marjorie Post Hutton Canteen, 1930s

BELOW: Marjorie and E.F. Hutton with friends in Palm Beach, Florida, 1920s

Portrait of Mrs. Hutton and Nedenia Hutton, by Giulio de Blaas. Italy, 1929. Oil on canvas

The Huttons eventually decided to sell the Burden Mansion, allowing for a fourteen-story apartment house to be erected in its place. Atop this towering structure sat their palatial triplex penthouse apartment, which at the time was considered to be the largest apartment ever built. In these elegant surroundings Marjorie continued to refine her collecting tastes, turning her attention to acquiring fine Sèvres porcelain, outstanding examples of French furniture, a collection of decorative gold boxes, and glittering objects and frames by the renowned jewelry firms of Cartier and later, Fabergé.

During this era of transformation for Marjorie, she and Hutton built both Mar-A-Lago, a 114-room estate in Palm Beach, and the *Hussar V*, a 316-foot sailing yacht with four masts. Her numerous residences served as repositories for her growing collection of luxury antique furnishings, while her father's cereal and prepared foods company continued to thrive.

The joy Marjorie found with her prominent life, ever-growing wealth, and elevated social status was muted by the stock market crash of October 1929. The years of the Great Depression sent throngs of starving men, women, and children into the streets of New York City. In line with C.W.'s lesson that wealth was a privilege best used to help others, Marjorie financed the Marjorie Post Hutton Canteen. There, women and children were served meals in a dignified manner unlike any other Depression-era soup kitchen. Marjorie also became actively involved in raising funds for the Women's Emergency Aid Committee of the Salvation Army. Charity luncheons, teas, and benefits replaced her once-lavish New York and Palm Beach parties.[4] Nonetheless, escalating tensions between the Huttons led to their divorce in 1935 after fifteen years of marriage.

In December of that year, Marjorie married Washington lawyer Joseph E. Davies. A few months later Davies was appointed to be the American ambassador to the Soviet Union. Marjorie's flourishing social skills and Davies's trusted relationship with President Franklin D. Roosevelt allowed them to gain the confidence of the Soviet government and with it, the special access that was granted to members of the diplomatic community. Although Marjorie acquired only the nucleus of what would become a remarkable collection of Russian art while in the Soviet Union, her passion for collecting Russian art was ignited and would continue to flourish for the next thirty-six years.

ABOVE: Marjorie with her granddaughter Marjorie Merriweather Durant and her daughter Nedenia on her wedding day to Joseph Davies, 1935

RIGHT: Marjorie and Joseph E. Davies. Courtesy Bentley Historical Library, University of Michigan

Spaso House, the residence of the American ambassador in Moscow, ca. 1937

Since 1918, when the Bolshevik Revolution ended the centuries-long Romanov reign with the assassination of Tsar Nicholas II and his family, the Soviet government had been selling treasures to raise the hard currency needed to finance its vast industrialization plans. The commission shops and state-run storerooms that had been established to sell these objects to Russians, Western art dealers, and foreign diplomats were well depleted by the time Marjorie arrived, but she discovered the fine and decorative arts of imperial Russia appealed to her taste for finely crafted objects.

At Spaso House, the American embassy in the Soviet Union, Marjorie enjoyed her role as diplomatic spouse, and she employed her skills as a gracious hostess to charm many new Soviet friends. When the Davies departed Moscow in June 1938, Madame Molotova, wife of Soviet diplomat Vyacheslav Molotov, presented Marjorie with a pair of vases selected from the ceramics museum. In an appropriate act of diplomacy, Marjorie gave the ceramics museum six Lenox plates with views of New York City, and she later sent additional pieces of American glass.

ESTATE 23

Marjorie at Tregaron, her first estate in Washington, D.C., 1940s

A LEGACY IN WASHINGTON

Life in the Soviet Union prepared Marjorie for the world of politics, diplomacy, and philanthropy that awaited her in Washington, D.C., when her husband's ambassadorial career ended with the declaration of World War II. Tregaron, their twenty-two-acre estate, became the backdrop for social functions that included politicians, heads of state, and visiting dignitaries. Davies remained in the spotlight as an expert in the field of Soviet-American relations, and Marjorie ensured her money was working for others through her involvement in war relief efforts. In 1942, for example, she claimed, "Since I have no son to give to the war, I will offer the *Sea Cloud*."[5] Marjorie rented her immense sailing yacht (formerly the *Hussar V*, which she had purchased with her former husband E.F. Hutton) to the United States Navy for one dollar per year.

The couple's social life prospered for nearly fifteen more years, as Marjorie's elegant parties, marked by her exquisite décor and warm Midwestern demeanor, became legendary. Tensions over Davies's falling status and ill health led to their divorce in 1955. Having sold her New York apartment, Marjorie remained committed to her life in Washington, and she promptly purchased Hillwood. As part of her seasonal rotation between winter in Palm Beach and summer in the Adirondacks, Hillwood served as her primary residence in the spring and fall for the rest of her life. Intending to leave Hillwood as her legacy, Marjorie ordered her architects and designers to refurbish the 1920s neo-Georgian house into a stately dwelling that could function as a home, a venue for grand entertaining, and a showcase for her collections to be enjoyed by future generations.

Marjorie shows her collection of French decorative arts to high school students, 1963

At Hillwood, Marjorie reigned as one of the top hostesses in the nation's capital, and her magnificent parties were inseparable from the political, business, and social fabric of Washington, D.C. With her full-time live-in and local staff, she organized memorable spring teas in the garden for hundreds of guests. A request to join her at a formal dinner at Hillwood was a highly prized invitation. Marjorie shared her life at Hillwood with her fourth husband, businessman Herbert May, from June 1958 to August 1964. Her first three marriages lasted from fourteen to twenty years, and following each wedding

ESTATE   25

ABOVE: A garden tea at Hillwood, 1960s

LEFT: Scampi was Marjorie's favorite dog at Hillwood.

Marjorie assumed her husband's last name. After her last divorce in 1964, she took the name Marjorie Merriweather Post once and for all.

Marjorie's sense of patriotism and passion for others continued to guide her life of philanthropy at Hillwood. In the 1960s and 1970s, crowning a nearly fifty-year commitment to supporting American soldiers and veterans of war, Marjorie invited Vietnam veterans, among them wounded Marines and Navy corpsmen from Bethesda Naval Hospital and patients from Walter Reed Army Medical Center, to enjoy live entertainment and

tea on the Lunar Lawn. She gave generously and often anonymously, and she actively participated in group efforts to raise money for the Salvation Army, American Red Cross, National Symphony Orchestra, Kennedy Center for the Performing Arts, Washington Ballet Guild, and other worthy organizations. The enduring effect of her generosity continues to be felt today at Hillwood.

[1] Hillwood Archives Microfilm, Post Collection, Reel 14, October 17, 1953.

[2] Marjorie Merriweather Post May, interview with John T. Mason, Jr., Oral History Research Office, Columbia University, February 13, 1964, 33–34. Hillwood Museum and Gardens Archives, Marjorie Merriweather Post Box, file no. 39.

[3] Nancy Rubin, *American Empress: The Life and Times of Marjorie Merriweather Post*, 2nd ed. (Lincoln, NE: iUniverse, 2004; New York: Villard Press, 1995), 101.

[4] Ibid., 180–81.

[5] Ibid., 276.

ABOVE: Marjorie hosting veterans of the Vietnam War at her estate, late 1960s

RIGHT: Hillwood employees presented Marjorie with a flagpole for the estate grounds in a ceremony on October 20, 1962.

Hillwood: Marjorie Merriweather Post's Living Legacy

When entering the grand entry hall at Hillwood today, visitors still experience the impressive welcome that was so carefully planned for diplomats, politicians, socialites, students, and friends of Marjorie Merriweather Post.

By the early 1950s, Marjorie was already considering creating a museum, and her divorce from Joseph Davies in 1955 moved this notion forward when she purchased Arbremont, a twenty-five-acre estate in northwest Washington, D.C. It was renamed Hillwood after the grand estate she had established with E.F. Hutton, her second husband, on Long Island in the 1920s. The new residence included a 1920s neo-Georgian mansion, which Marjorie intended to use both as a comfortable home and as a place to showcase her growing art collections.

An extensive renovation, undertaken by the architectural firm of Alexander McIlvaine and the interior design firm of French and Company, transformed Hillwood into a stately mansion perfectly suited for the scale of elegant entertaining for which Marjorie was well known. From the time she purchased the estate until she welcomed her first guests two years later in 1957, Hillwood underwent a dramatic transformation. The kitchen was enlarged and outfitted with the most modern equipment available. The roof was raised to accommodate a third story, a wing for entertaining was added, bathrooms were updated, imported period woodwork was installed, and display cases were built to show off collections of Russian and French objects. As the culmination of a lifetime of collecting art and creating stately homes, Hillwood combined a regal European elegance with all of the modern amenities necessary for life in the 1950s.

[The estate was] the proper setting in Washington for the kind of perfection of craftsmanship that came out of the palaces of czars, the chateau of Mme. Pompadour or the estate of an English lord.
—Betty Beale, *Washington Star*, 1957

Porte cochere
© Maxwell MacKenzie

Entry hall

ENTRY HALL

Every visit to Hillwood begins in the columned entry hall. In this two-story reception area, walls are faced with plaster to simulate the appearance and feel of limestone. Exquisite furnishings and historic objects introduce the dual interests that guided Marjorie's passion for collecting: the decorative and fine arts of both eighteenth-century France and eighteenth- and nineteenth-century imperial Russia.

My two major interests have been the art of 18th-century France and that of Imperial Russia.… French 18th-century art was my earlier interest and the Russian collection only started when I was en poste in Russia.… As the influence of French artists and artisans was very strong in old Saint Petersburg and Moscow, it seems quite natural that these two artistic expressions should be brought together here.[1]

Lining the regal staircase, with its French wrought-iron and gilt-bronze railing, are imposing portraits of the tsars and tsarinas of the Russian monarchy. Catherine the Great, who was a self-declared "defender of the arts and sciences" and has been credited with modernizing Russia, especially fascinated Marjorie. A powerful full-length portrait of the tsarina commands the stairway in the entry hall. Along the walls flanking the library, two commodes, or chests of drawers, attributed to Jean-Henri Riesener, the German-born official cabinetmaker to Louis XVI and Marie Antoinette, attest to Marjorie's discerning taste for superbly crafted furnishings. A rare French rock crystal chandelier, believed to have once hung in the Gatchina Palace in Russia, dramatically illuminates

Russian porcelain room

the space. It is also the embodiment of Marjorie's dual interests in France and Russia.

Just off the entry hall is the ladies powder room, still delightfully decorated in a 1950s style. Nearby, male visitors were welcome to drop off their overcoats in the men's room, where Marjorie had artfully hung William-Adolphe Bouguereau's *Night*, a painting of a partially nude woman apparently floating over the seacoast.

RUSSIAN PORCELAIN ROOM

In the Russian porcelain room, Marjorie displayed a captivating array of imperial porcelain that she had brought back from the Soviet Union in the 1930s. An imperial double-headed eagle, inlaid in the center of the wood floor, forms a fitting backdrop for the Russian glass and porcelain on view. The most prominent pieces displayed here were once part of four military order services that Catherine the Great commissioned in the late eighteenth century. Honored for their government and military service, knights of the various orders dined on these pieces when they were invited to the Winter Palace on the feast day of their order's patron saint.

Marjorie designed the size, appearance, and function of the display cases in this room and all the others on the first floor. In planning the renovations for Hillwood, the forward-thinking collector requested that built-in, lighted display cases, replete with pull-out trays with object labels, be included in almost every room. Although the label trays are not in use today, Marjorie's desire to educate visitors about her collections is now carried on through docent-led and audio tours.

ESTATE 31

Icon room, 1970s

Fabergé Imperial Easter egg and clock in the Icon room

ICON ROOM

More than four hundred glistening chalices, silver-covered icons, and splendid Fabergé objects are on view in this intimate setting tucked among Hillwood's stately rooms. While designing Hillwood with a public audience in mind, Marjorie realized she needed an appropriate space for displaying small precious objects and liturgical treasures. In this collector's cabinet she placed beautifully crafted objects, preferably those with an imperial provenance, and pieces by the firm of the Russian jeweler Carl Fabergé—from clocks, cane handles, and picture frames to imperial Easter eggs.

Both the midnight blue *Twelve Monogram Easter Egg* (see p. 77) and the pink *Catherine the Great Easter Egg* (see p. 76) were gifts from Tsar Nicholas II to his mother, Dowager Empress Maria Fedorovna. The pale green bowenite clock was modeled after an eighteenth-century English timepiece that also belonged to Maria Fedorovna. Portraits of her son, Nicholas II, and her daughter-in-law, Empress Alexandra, adorn the sides.

ESTATE 33

French drawing room

FRENCH DRAWING ROOM

Elegant evenings at Hillwood were spent in this sumptuous room, resplendent with Beauvais tapestries, Sèvres porcelain, glistening gold boxes, and chairs upholstered with Gobelins tapestry (see p. 60). Distinguished guests, from diplomats, politicians, and members of the Washington social set to Marjorie's family and friends, met here for cocktails. Many of those who enjoyed Marjorie's hospitality are seen in photographs on the grand piano. In keeping with her wish, fresh floral arrangements grace the mansion in perpetuity.

The painted and gilt wood paneling—imported from a Paris mansion dating to the reign of King Louis XVI (1774–92)—provides a majestic backdrop for Marjorie's passion for eighteenth-century France. Exceptional pieces include an intricate roll-top desk crafted by the renowned father-and-son team of Abraham and David Roentgen (see p. 59). Another is the gilt wood and leather swivel chair crafted by Claude I Sené, a member of one of the most famous dynasties of Parisian chairmakers. It bears the stamp of the Garde Meuble de la Reine, the office in charge of supplying furnishings for Queen Marie Antoinette's private apartments. The chair's low back and swivel seat would have made it easier to powder the queen's hair.

The French drawing room was one of several spaces in the house designed to connect harmoniously with the gardens just beyond its walls. In nice weather, the double doors were opened to flow to the French parterre outside.

Swivel chair and rug in the French drawing room

PAVILION

Marjorie built the pavilion to accommodate large parties and to provide space for after-dinner entertainment. First-run movies were projected onto a screen that drops from the ceiling over the piano at the far end of the room. Rows of petite sofas were equipped with pop-up trays to hold drinks and snacks. (The butler prepared cocktails at the wet bar located on the way into the pavilion.)

Two large paintings dominate the pavilion. *Portrait of Countess Samoilova* by Karl Briullov (see p. 78), resplendent with rich textures and opulent colors, represents a time when Russians strove to emulate European aesthetic tastes and cultural values. In contrast, *A Boyar Wedding Feast* by Konstantin Makovsky (see p. 79) embodies the Russian revival style that celebrated traditions before Peter the Great's push for Westernization. Together, these paintings demonstrate a major shift in Russia's artistic expression and national identity in the nineteenth century.

Other objects on view are also largely Russian in origin. The dishes that flank the entrance are elaborate examples of the plates traditionally used to greet guests with bread and salt. Atop the piano are photographs of Russia's last imperial family: Tsar Nicholas II, Tsarina Alexandra, and their children.

Pavilion

FIRST FLOOR LIBRARY

Paneled with eighteenth-century pine cut and carved in England, the library provided Marjorie with a cozy setting to entertain a few friends or family in front of the fireplace. Among her personal touches in the room is a portrait of her father, C.W. Post, and at the other end hangs a portrait of her mother, Ella Merriweather Post. Cartier frames that Marjorie commissioned perfectly complement an assortment of family photographs and miniatures.

ABOVE: First floor library today

LEFT: First floor library, 1962

ABOVE: Dining room

RIGHT: Detail of the hardstone mosaic tabletop

DINING ROOM

Marjorie's sense of perfection in all things—from the splendid décor to the place settings to the dinner service—came together in the dining room. The early eighteenth-century oak paneling, featuring such rococo motifs as billowing scrolls and graceful long-tailed birds, sets a lively tone for this French-inspired room. Four large Dutch paintings of hunting scenes add a stately touch, and a nineteenth-century Aubusson carpet, a gift from Napoleon III to Emperor Maximillian of Mexico, enlivens the floor.

The central focus of the room is the magnificent table, with a mosaic top composed of eleven different types of stone. It can comfortably accommodate up to thirty guests. Commissioned in 1927 from the Opificio delle Pietre Dure—the most celebrated hardstone workshop in Florence, Italy—the table was originally designed for Mar-A-Lago, the lavish Palm Beach estate Marjorie built with her second husband, financier E.F. Hutton. A provision in her will called for the table to be moved from Florida to Hillwood following her death.

Today, table settings in the dining room and the adjacent breakfast room are regularly changed with porcelain, glass, and flatware selected from Marjorie's extensive collection of French, Russian, and other historic services. Three or four times each year, the settings are carefully chosen to evoke the season, reinterpret a special exhibition, or recreate a grand dinner party.

As in Marjorie's time, the floral arrangements in the dining room and throughout the house come primarily from Hillwood's cutting gardens and greenhouses. Staff horticulturists and floral designers often consult historic photographs to create modern-day variations of the arrangements that were enjoyed in the rooms during her years at Hillwood.

BREAKFAST ROOM

Off the stately dining room sits a charming, light-filled space, perfect for Marjorie's less formal lunches, afternoon teas, or intimate dinners. With its view over the expansive Lunar Lawn, the breakfast room visually blends with the glorious outdoor spaces. The design of this space recalls the breakfast room in Marjorie's former New York City apartment. In fact, the bronze metalwork that lines the space came directly from that fashionable Upper East Side residence.

Marjorie had the table set for four at all times, even when she was dining alone. Today, place settings in the breakfast room are changed several times each year as a way to display her diverse collection. Vibrant floral arrangements enliven the room and show off the bounty of the cutting gardens and greenhouses.

Breakfast room

FRENCH PORCELAIN ROOM

Much to their surprise and delight, guests at Hillwood were often served from the valuable Russian imperial and French porcelain that Marjorie acquired. An alcove off the dining room was reserved for displaying special pieces from her prized collection of Sèvres porcelain.

Marjorie began purchasing French porcelain in the 1920s, and she retained a lifelong love for the famed *blue celeste*, or "heavenly blue," pieces in particular. One large tureen made in 1754 (see p. 62) probably came from the first complete service that the Sèvres factory ever produced. Its curving shapes, reminiscent of eighteenth-century architecture, became a hallmark of Sèvres design.

Also on view are a cup and saucer with a portrait of Benjamin Franklin to commemorate his time in Paris solidifying French support of American independence. A pair of cups decorated with rebuses, or word and picture puzzles, delight with translations reading "she is ravishingly beautiful" as well as "and he possesses you."

TOP: Cup and Saucer with Rebus. France, 1788. Sèvres Porcelain Manufactory. Soft paste porcelain

LEFT: Cup with Portrait of Benjamin Franklin. France, ca. 1779. Sèvres Porcelain Manufactory. Soft paste porcelain

KITCHEN AND PANTRY

Despite her passion for French eighteenth-century interior design, Marjorie appreciated modern-day conveniences in the kitchen. Her staff was fully equipped to prepare and serve memorable meals for intimate dinners or large garden parties. The kitchen's state-of-the-art appliances from the 1950s include multiple Hobart standing mixers, a Globe Gravity Feed meat slicer, an Oster Touch-a-Matic combination can opener and juicer, and a West Bend percolator capable of brewing fifty-five cups of coffee. Next to the heavy-duty stainless steel counters are a nine-burner Magic Chef stove and a large Sta-Kold freezer—a nod to Marjorie's ties to the frozen food industry.

Every feature needed to ease work for Marjorie's staff was found in the pantry. Modern green Geneva steel cabinets that once stored everyday services line the walls. A dumbwaiter from the secure storage in the basement was used to transport precious porcelain and glass, and silver was stored in a walk-in safe. Timers built into the cabinets made efficiency a priority.

OPPOSITE: Kitchen

TOP: Sta-Kold freezers

ABOVE: Dumbwaiter in the pantry

RIGHT: Staff dining room in the 1960s

STAFF DINING ROOM AND LOUNGE

Ever mindful of the well-being of her staff, Marjorie took great care to provide comfortable accommodations for them. The house alone had sixteen to eighteen staff members, including a butler, footmen, and maids, who received housing and meals as part of their compensation. Adjacent to the kitchen is a recreation of the rooms where the staff dined and gathered around a portable Zenith television. An organization chart details the flow of people required to maintain the flawless style of living and entertaining that Marjorie enjoyed during her seasons at Hillwood and at her other residences.

With its informal furnishings and proximity to the kitchen, the staff dining room was a popular gathering place for young guests looking for a laugh and a snack of dinner party leftovers.

My brothers and I used to hang out here with the staff or watch tv. It was a place where we could go and roughhouse and not get in trouble.
—George Iverson, great-grandson of Marjorie Merriweather Post

ESTATE 43

Portraits in the second floor hall

SECOND FLOOR HALL

The transitional space between public and private lives offers a microcosm of Marjorie's collection, with stunning examples of French, Russian, and English decorative arts intermingling with Old Master paintings. A display case at the top of the stairs contains English painted enamels. Less expensive than gilt containers, these colorful objects were popular among the European elite in the eighteenth and nineteenth centuries. Russian porcelain, made in both imperial and privately owned factories, is also carefully arranged throughout the open balcony area. A portrait of Marjorie and her daughter Nedenia Hutton (actress Dina Merrill) painted by Giulio de Blaas in 1929 hangs on the wall. Marjorie wears a large emerald brooch by Cartier that is often displayed in the special jewelry area of the closets. An exceptional portrait of Mrs. Thomas Heron by George Romney hangs directly opposite it, while Marguerite Gérard's *Beloved Child* is on view farther down the hall.

Icon. Russia, ca. 1700. Tempera on wood with gilding

RUSSIAN SACRED ARTS GALLERY

What were once staff quarters is now a peaceful gallery dedicated to sacred Russian Orthodox ecclesiastical objects: icons created for the veneration of saints, elaborate chalices used for communion, and vestments, chalice covers, altar cloths, and other religious textiles. (Low light levels protect the textiles from deterioration.)

The most magnificent piece—a gold chalice (see p. 70) that Catherine the Great commissioned in 1791 as part of a communion set—stands in splendor in the center of the room. The dazzling nuptial crown (see p. 68) that Empress Alexandra wore in 1894 during her wedding to Nicholas II is also on display here. Bands of diamonds are sewn onto the velvet-covered supports of this orb-shaped wedding crown, and a cross of six larger, old mine-cut diamonds surmounts it. Other objects focus on the private use of icons in the Russian home.

SECOND FLOOR LIBRARY

The second floor library resembles an English country house, right down to the Chippendale gaming table. Its wood paneling, furnishings, and sporting paintings repeat the eighteenth-century British flavor of the larger library on the first floor. Sir Oswald Birley's portrait of Eleanor Close Barzin, Marjorie's second daughter, in a riding costume presides over one end of the room. Above the English mantel on the opposite end hangs Frank O. Salisbury's portrait of an elegant Marjorie Merriweather Post in the 1940s.

Designed as an extension of the Adam bedroom, this cozy library offers an alternative to the formality of the first floor rooms. A grand view of the Lunar Lawn and Rock Creek Park greeted guests, although curtains now closed to protect precious objects and furnishings obscure the intended view of the Washington Monument.

Second floor library

ESTATE 45

ADAM BEDROOM

Named for the English neoclassical style of decoration popularized by Robert and John Adam in the late eighteenth and early nineteenth centuries, this bedroom features ornamental plasterwork on the ceiling that echoes the design of the carpet gracing the floor. Antique English furniture, Wedgwood jasperware ice pails on the mantel, and other furnishings complete the Adam-style treatment of the room.

In a portrait by Frank O. Salisbury from 1946 above the fireplace, Marjorie wears a beautiful Cartier sapphire, diamond, and platinum necklace.

LEFT: *Portrait of Marjorie Merriweather Post*, by Frank O. Salisbury. United States, 1946. Oil on canvas

BELOW: Adam bedroom

Marjorie's bedroom

MARJORIE MERRIWEATHER POST'S BEDROOM SUITE

Perfection in pink describes the personal spaces of Marjorie's bedroom suite. A pink and gold color scheme governs, from the Louis XVI canopied bed to the dresses that Marjorie's daughters Adelaide and Eleanor wear in the portrait by Pierre Tartoué.

Over the fireplace is Douglas Chandor's portrait of Marjorie, which was hung there after her death. Chandor died before completing the work, leaving the hands unfinished. In the nearby display cases are *étuis*—small containers to carry sewing or toilet items—snuffboxes, and other objects made primarily of bloodstone, Marjorie's birthstone. The feeling of European opulence extends out the window to the view of the French parterre, the "garden room" purposely situated below.

Marjorie's dressing room

A nucleus of activity at Hillwood was the dressing room, which served as Marjorie's morning office. There she took her breakfast, discussed menus with the butler, reviewed correspondence with her secretary, and otherwise ordered her day. The walls lined with family photographs underscore the deeply personal feel of this private space.

Equally personal are the bold choices that Marjorie made for the bathroom in her bedroom suite. "Mamie Pink," a shade named after the favorite color of First Lady Mamie Eisenhower, was wildly popular in the 1950s. Pink was also one of Marjorie's longtime favorite colors, and she used it liberally in her private rooms.

A hallway off the dressing room now displays select pieces of Marjorie's splendid jewelry. Here, presentations of her sparkling gems and custom-made shoes change throughout the year. Vintage gowns and ensembles provide an enlightening glimpse into the evolution of fashion during Marjorie's lifetime. A case of drawers contains delicate pieces from her extensive collection of European lace.

TOP: The "Mamie Pink" bathroom

RIGHT: Marjorie's clothes in a closet of her bedroom suite

BEHIND THE SCENES

Several spaces at Hillwood that firmly root the estate in the modern era of the 1950s and 1960s are available only through special access. In the basement is one of four fallout shelters that Marjorie had built across the estate in the 1960s. Now refurbished, one pink-walled shelter is stocked with a supply of goods, including General Foods products. The film projection booth above the pavilion houses the original movie equipment, complete with anamorphic lenses for Cinemascope projection. And the massage room on the second floor, created for Marjorie's hairdressing, still displays the original hair dryers and permanent wave machine used for the final touches of her impeccably groomed appearance.

[1] Marjorie Merriweather Post, *Notes on Hillwood* (Washington, D.C.: Hillwood, 1970), 1.

LEFT: Original hair dryers and a permanent wave machine used for Marjorie's hairdressing

TOP: Fallout shelter, 1960s

ABOVE: A supply of goods in the pink fallout shelter

OPPOSITE: Marjorie Merriweather Post, ca. 1940s

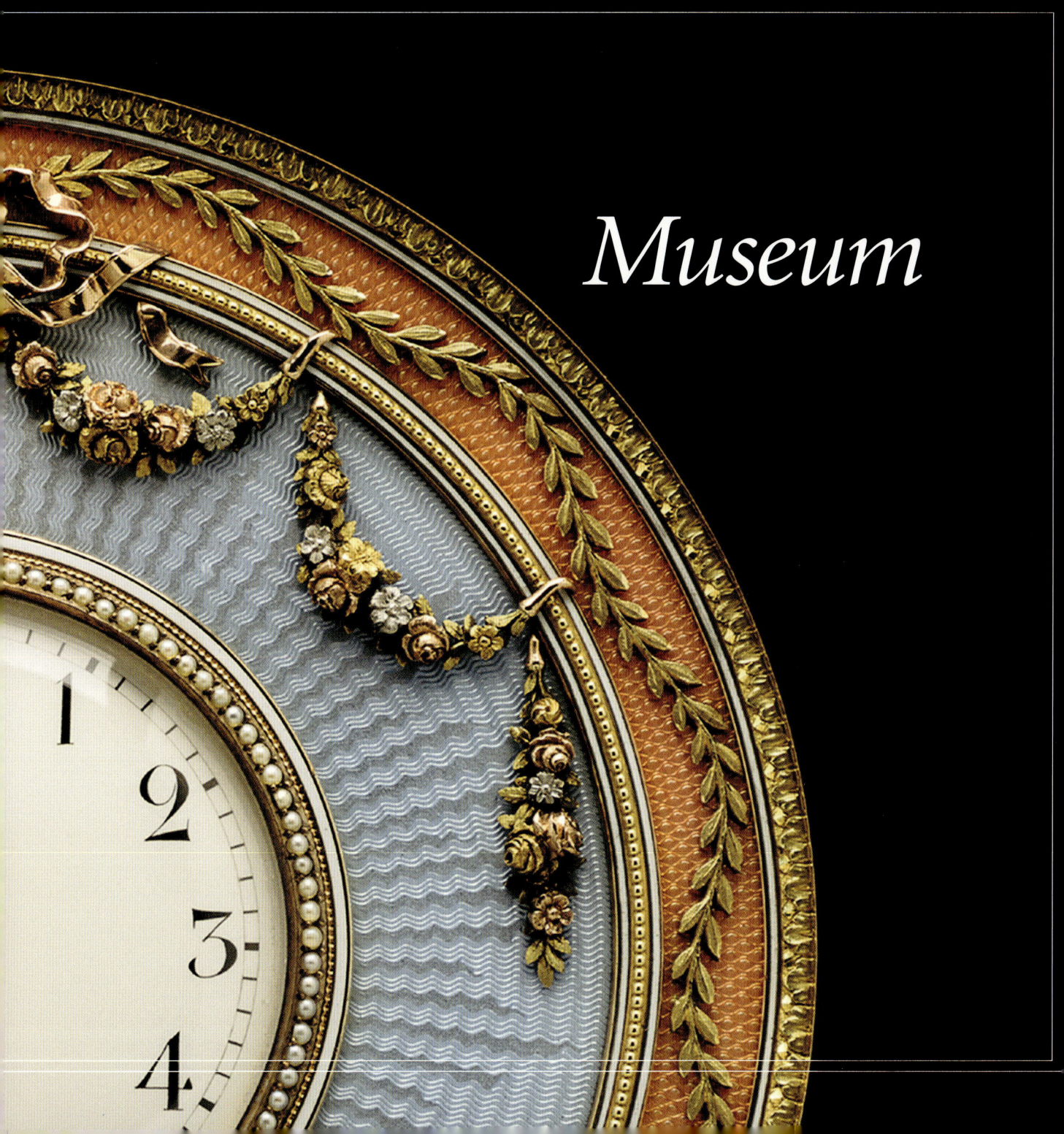

Museum

When I began collecting, I did it for the joy of it, and it was only as the collection grew and such great interest was evidenced by others that I came to the realization that the collection should belong to the country.

Marjorie Merriweather Post, 1970

PREVIOUS: Table clock, Russia, 1898–1903. Design by firm of Carl Fabergé. Mikhail Perkhin, workmaster. Silver, enamel, ivory, clockworks, gold, pearls, diamonds

OPPOSITE: *Vase with African Birds* (detail). France, 1882. Sèvres Porcelain Manufactory. Porcelain, ormolu, bronze

Collecting with Passion, Connoisseurship, and Style

Here let Art be used
To soften commerce;
And Music to rest the soul
From the tire of the day.[1]

—From Postum Cereal Company, introduction to the collections of C.W. Post

Marjorie's first visions of a personal art collection go back to the gallery her father created in his corporate offices in Battle Creek, Michigan, in the early 1900s. His eclectic display of uplifting works of art and objects from faraway civilizations surely felt transporting to the workers at the Postum factory. In an act of great prescience, Marjorie paid tribute to her father's vision for improving life by carefully re-editing the first guide to his galleries in 1954, three years before she welcomed visitors to her own museum of sorts. The mission of C.W.'s gallery made a powerful impression on young Marjorie and shaped the spirit of her collecting legacy decades later.

Here and there are brilliant examples of Venetian carving, bits of carved inscriptions from the ruins of Rome, specimens of intricate Moorish art, and finely wrought suits of armor, together with interesting Indian and prehistoric objects from the Southwest, all of which combine with the pictures on the walls to hold the visitor entranced in the unusual atmosphere of the place.[2]

—From Postum Cereal Company, introduction to the collections of C.W. Post

Eventually shying away from the eclecticism and clutter of the late Victorian style of her childhood, Marjorie progressively carved her own collecting path. Over the years she became a renowned collector of French and European decorative arts and a pioneer in the field of Russian imperial art.

From the early 1920s through the late 1960s, Marjorie collected in a steady and relentless fashion. Her legacy of acquiring more than seventeen thousand works of art, jewelry, and personal apparel now attracts visitors and scholars from around the world to Hillwood.

FRENCH COLLECTION

Marjorie grounded her collecting in the grand tradition of French art and architecture that swept the United States at the turn of the twentieth century. This interest stirred her to buy French eighteenth-century furniture, tapestries, gold boxes, and royal porcelains manufactured by Sèvres. By the mid-1920s she had accumulated such large numbers of important objects that art dealer Sir Joseph Duveen coaxed her into having them catalogued. Duveen, in Marjorie's words, was the most important man in her life besides her father. By the end of the decade she had developed a keen eye and a set of criteria for collecting: the works of art had to be aesthetically pleasing, well designed, skillfully executed, and historically relevant.

OPPOSITE: Military Presentation Cup. Russia, 1834. Made by Johann Christian Barbé. Gold

> ONLY A COLLECTOR OF DISCRIMINATING AND FASTIDIOUS TASTE COULD HAVE GATHERED SUCH CHOICE EXAMPLES OF FRENCH ÉBÉNISTERIE.[3]
> —Frank Jewett Mather, art critic, ca. 1927

These words, in the prologue of her privately printed catalogue from circa 1927, eloquently describe the manner in which Marjorie collected French furniture. All the pieces she so lovingly acquired can be viewed today in the environment that was specially created for them at Hillwood. Featured among them are two chests of drawers, or commodes, by Jean-Henri Riesener. Appointed *ébéniste du roi* (king's cabinetmaker) in 1774, Riesener supplied the court with hundreds of pieces of

LEFT: Swivel chair. France, ca. 1785. Designed by Claude I Séné. Gilt wood, leather

BELOW: Commode with pastoral marquetry. France, ca. 1775. Designed by Jean-Henri Riesener. Wood marquetry, gilt bronze, marble

Roll-top desk. Germany, 1765–70. Designed by Abraham and David Roentgen. Wood marquetry, mother of pearl, gilt bronze, steel, leather, glass

furniture. The commode, illustrated opposite, is of the same model that Riesener delivered to the bedchamber of Louis XVI at Versailles the very year he was appointed. The highly pictorial and naturalistic marquetry reveals the superior skill of this master *ébéniste*.

Another piece with royal connections is a swivel chair by Claude I Sené. This singular chair for a dressing table belonged to Queen Marie Antoinette. Branded with the stamp of her personal furniture repository, the Garde Meuble de la Reine, it has the peculiarity of being designed for styling and powdering the queen's hair. Its swivel seat and low back could readily accommodate the elaborate hairdos of the period.

A stellar piece among the furniture at Hillwood is a roll-top desk. It is the work of the German father-and-son team of Abraham and David Roentgen, owners of the most important furniture shop outside France. A tour de force of marquetry and mechanical devices, the desk contains more than forty secret compartments, and it was one of Marjorie's most treasured pieces. It was long thought to have been made for Marie Antoinette, but recent research has revealed it was created for Princess Maria Antonia of Bavaria and Regent of Saxony, a clever stateswoman with a penchant for composing music and writing. The iconography of the desk, featuring musical instruments and sheet music, clearly alludes to this.

Collecting tapestries went hand in hand with Marjorie's acquisitions of furniture. At the instigation of her mentor Sir Joseph Duveen, she took classes on the art of textiles and tapestry at the Metropolitan Museum of Art. Such initiation opened up a new world of collecting and decorating possibilities in the grand manner of such discerning collectors as J.P. Morgan and Henry Clay Frick.

MUSEUM 59

ABOVE: Armchair from a furniture suite (one of twelve). France, 1784–86. Tapestries designed by Louis Tessier and woven by the Gobelins Tapestry Manufactory. Gilt wood, wool, silk

TOP LEFT: Heart-shaped box with Dutch scenes. Paris, 1756–62. Box by François Guillaume Tiron. Scenes after David Teniers II. Gold, enamel

TOP RIGHT: Heart-shaped box with flowers. Paris, 1756–62. Attributed to François Guillaume Tiron. Gold, enamel

The walls of the French drawing room are covered with Beauvais tapestries after designs by François Boucher. One represents Italian feasts and the other two are part of a series on the Loves of Gods that the famed court painter designed for the Beauvais manufactory. In line with the decorating trend of the mid-twentieth century, they are fitted into wooden frames, rather than being allowed to hang freely as they traditionally would have done.

Another important set of tapestries in the collection includes an imposing suite of chairs covered with Gobelins tapestries. Unlike Beauvais, which accepted both private and royal commissions, the Gobelins factory worked almost exclusively for the crown. These chair covers were a gift from King Louis XVI and Marie Antoinette to Prince Henry of Prussia, a Francophile who, on his departure from his visit to France in 1784, proffered, "I have passed half my life in wishing to see France—I shall pass the other half in regretting it."[4]

The large collection of gold boxes and objects of *vertu* at Hillwood testifies to Marjorie's sustained interest in precious objects with historical associations. Author Edith Wharton commented on the prevalent accumulation of bibelots as "the voluptuousness of acquiring things one may do without."[5] Wharton's words convey the eternal allure that these small creations

TOP: Shell-shaped snuffbox. Paris, 1722–27. Mother of pearl, gold, enamel

ABOVE: Box with *Catherine the Great in the Guise of Minerva*. Paris, 1781–82. Sold by Charles-Raymond Granchez at Au Petit Dunkerke. Gold, *verre églomisé*

TOP: Snuffbox. Paris, 1774. Designed by Charles Le Bastier. Gold, enamel

ABOVE: Round box with leopard print. Paris, 1783–84. Designed by Louis Lacarrière. Sold by Charles-Raymond Granchez at Au Petit Dunkerke. Gold, enamel

they were intended as tokens of love or as a wedding present. The shell-shaped snuffbox is one of the earliest boxes in the collection, dating to the early 1720s. The leopard-skin box and a snuffbox decorated with a couple presenting an offering to Cupid at the altar of love represent the apogee of the Parisian gold box during the neoclassical period. Charles Le Bastier designed the box with borders lavishly decorated with restrained classical motifs and clusters of instruments on grounds of vivid pink and lapis blue. The leopard-skin box, a creation of the fashionable Parisian shop Au Petit Dunkerke, would have been *au courant* during the 1770s, when the trend of decorating with velvets printed to imitate a patterned animal skin was popular.

Commemorative boxes were a lavish way to mark important political events in the eighteenth century. The box with *Catherine the Great in the Guise of Minerva* also comes from Au Petit Dunkerke. The shop's shrewd owner, Charles-Raymond Granchez, was always ready to market pieces in connection with important current affairs, in this case the visit of Grand Duke Paul, the son of the Russian empress, and his wife, Maria Fedorovna, to Paris in 1782.

have held for collectors over the centuries. Marjorie bought many of her gold boxes in the 1920s and 1930s. These ornate French boxes set the tone for her collection of *vertu* in general, including her later works by Carl Fabergé and even her jewels by Cartier. They epitomize her taste for beautifully crafted items and her affinity for precious materials and small objects that embody the civility and frivolity of the Ancien Régime.

A pair of heart-shaped boxes are among the rarest pieces in the collection, for no other boxes of this particular shape are known. Their heart forms suggest

Sèvres porcelain was another of Marjorie's early collecting passions. She was particularly attracted to the turquoise blue and pink wares that have become the hallmark colors of the French royal porcelain manufacturer. What began as a private enterprise in Vincennes in 1753 soon counted as one of its main shareholders King Louis XV, who became involved through his mistress, Madame de Pompadour. This collection has the unmistakable imprint of her preference for classical and beautifully crafted works of art.

ABOVE: Soup tureen (detail). 1754.
Vincennes Porcelain Manufactory. Soft paste porcelain

RIGHT: Plate from the Rohan Service (one of thirty). 1771.
Sèvres Porcelain Manufactory. Soft paste porcelain

OPPOSITE: Vase (Cuvette Mahon). 1757.
Sèvres Porcelain Manufactory. Soft paste porcelain

Most of the public spaces on the first floor of Hillwood feature Sèvres porcelain. Among the earliest pieces is a highly sculptural soup tureen made at Vincennes, the first location of the factory before it moved to Sèvres in 1756. Two years prior to this move, the first service in deep turquoise blue—a coveted color that became a hallmark of Sèvres—was completed and delivered to King Louis XV.

Marjorie used historical Sèvres services at her dining table. The most lavish set was commissioned by Cardinal Prince de Rohan, a spendthrift prelate who wanted to celebrate his appointment as envoy to the court of Vienna in 1771. Each plate features his cypher in two tones of gold, an extravagant and costly feature of this historical service.

Outstanding among Hillwood's many exceptional vases is the *Cuvette Mahon*, with its unusual pink color. The Duke of Orléans purchased it at the sale held each Christmas in the king's private apartments at Versailles. Its name refers to the town of Mahon on the island of Minorca, which the French captured in 1756 in what was celebrated as one of the great triumphs of the Seven Years' War.

ABOVE: Plate from the South American Birds Service. 1819–20. Pauline de Courcelles/Madame Knip, painter; J.F.C. Leloi, border designer. Sèvres Porcelain Manufactory. Soft paste porcelain

LEFT: *Vase with African Birds*. 1822. Sèvres Porcelain Manufactory. Porcelain, gilt bronze

OPPOSITE: Plate with *Ballet Russes* Bacchante figure. 1913. Sèvres Porcelain Manufactory. Hard paste porcelain

The *Vase with African Birds* of 1822 and the plate from the South American Birds Service are superb examples of the enduring creativity of the Sèvres factory after the French Revolution. Pauline de Courcelles (Madame Knip), an accomplished woman artist of the time who specialized in painting birds on vellum, painted these specimens by hand. Almost a century later, the *Ballet Russes* plates of 1913 not only capture the vibrancy of the dance company that took Paris by storm in the early 1910s, but they also attest to the continuing appeal of Sèvres porcelain.

Paintings at Hillwood serve mostly as backdrops to the decorative arts that take center stage. Nevertheless, a group of distinguished canvases rounds out the

ABOVE: *Portrait of the Duchess of Parma and Her Daughter Isabelle*, by Jean-Marc Nattier. 1750. Oil on canvas

RIGHT: *Portrait of Empress Eugénie*, by Franz Xavier Winterhalter. 1857. Oil on canvas

OPPOSITE: *The Beloved Child (L'Enfant chérie)*, by Marguerite Gérard and Jean-Honoré Fragonard. Ca. 1790. Oil on canvas

collection. *Portrait of the Duchess of Parma and Her Daughter Isabelle,* by the court painter Jean-Marc Nattier, depicts the eldest daughter of Louis XV visiting her father at Fontainebleau. In another portrait Franz Xavier Winterhalter captured the beauty and glamour of Empress Eugénie a year after the birth of her son. Seated outdoors, the empress fills the canvas with her large straw hat and white ruffled dress trimmed with blue ribbons. The domestic genre scene depicted in *Beloved Child* is the charming and idealized work of Marguerite Gérard. Not only was she one of the few woman painters in the eighteenth century, but she was also the sister-in-law and pupil of the great artist Jean-Honoré Fragonard, who some experts believe contributed to this painting.

RUSSIAN COLLECTION

The eighteen months (1937–38) that Marjorie spent in the Soviet Union with her husband, Ambassador Joseph Davies, had a profound effect on her collecting interests. It sparked her passion for Russian art, an almost uncharted area that few had tread with such intensity. By the late 1960s she had assembled an immense cross-section of imperial Russian art, including icons, ecclesiastical objects, pieces by Fabergé, metalwork, enamel, and massive amounts of porcelain.

One truly exceptional object is the nuptial crown that the Soviets sold at Christie's London in 1927. It did not enter the Post collection until three decades later, in 1966, after being in the possession of other American owners. Worn by Tsarina Alexandra at her wedding to Nicholas II in 1894, the crown is the only piece of imperial regalia outside Russia today.

The commission shops and state-run storerooms that had been established by the Soviet government to sell unwanted objects and to raise much-needed funds were well depleted by the time Marjorie and Joe Davies arrived in 1937. Marjorie was still able to buy ecclesiastical objects, icons, and porcelains. She recounted that in one commission shop, to which they had special access as members of the diplomatic community, she discovered religious textiles and liturgical silver. The chalices were so tarnished that she was uncertain if they were actually silver. She paid for the chalices by weight, approximately five cents per gram. Contrary to the general belief that she bought most of her Russian art in the Soviet Union, Marjorie purchased only a small nucleus of her collection while in Moscow.

ABOVE: Display of chalices in the Icon room, 1950s

OPPOSITE: Nuptial Crown. Russia, 1884. Silver, diamonds, velvet

She acquired her most outstanding pieces of ecclesiastical art in the West, years after the objects had been sold by the Soviets. A chalice by Iver Windfeldt Buch, a masterful example of eighteenth-century goldsmithing, came from Wartski's in London. It was commissioned by Catherine the Great, who provided the diamonds, cameos, and intaglios from her own collection. In 1791 the empress presented it to the monastery of Saint Alexander Nevsky in memory of Grigory Potemkin, her favorite courtier.

Chalice, designed by Swedish goldsmith Iver Windfeldt Buch. St. Petersburg, 1791. Gold, diamonds, chalcedony, bloodstone, nephrite, carnelian, cast glass

LEFT: *St. George with Deisis, Saints, and Martyrs.* 16th century. Tempera on wood

ABOVE: *Iverskaia Mother of God.* Moscow, 1875–1900. Pavel Ovchinnikov, *oklad.* Tempera on wood, silver gilt, filigree enamel, seed pearls

The icons that Marjorie bought in the commission shops of Moscow mirrored the vast range of religious objects that had been cast adrift by the social upheavals of the Russian Revolution. Among the early examples at Hillwood is the large icon of *Saint George Slaying the Dragon.* Later icons from the eighteenth and nineteenth centuries are adorned with ornate silver covers *(oklads).* They exemplify both icon paintings and luxury decorative arts, as can be seen in the icon of the *Iverskaia Mother of God.* Made by the Ovchinnikov firm in Moscow, this revered icon is enlivened with colorful enamels on silver, while the image of the Mother of God is covered with seed pearls.

MUSEUM 71

Among the most important pieces Marjorie purchased in Moscow is a Renaissance-style cabinet of ebonized wood set with lapis lazuli panels and mounted in gilt bronze. Tsar Alexander II and his wife, Maria Alexandrovna, presented it to his brother, Grand Duke Constantin, and his wife on their twenty-fifth wedding anniversary in 1873.

Porcelains were one of Marjorie's primary interests and are today the main feature of the Hillwood collection. The Russian order services were large banquet settings commissioned by Catherine the Great from Russia's Gardner factory for the knights of the orders of Saint Alexander Nevsky, Saint Alexander, Saint Andrew, Saint George, and Saint Vladimir. Marjorie amassed enough of each of these services to be able to entertain her awed guests at the dinner table. She also collected several grand porcelain vases of the kind she had seen in Russian palaces. Quite often they were decorated with copies of Old Master and European paintings in the collection of the Hermitage. One such vase is illustrated with *The Herring Seller*, a painting by Gerrit Dou.

LEFT: Cabinet. St. Petersburg, 1873. Designed by Ippolit Monigetti; made by Nichols and Plinke. Ebonized wood, lapis lazuli, gilt bronze

RIGHT: Ice Cup from the Order of St. George Dessert Service. Verbilki, 18th century. Gardner Factory. Hard paste porcelain

72 HILLWOOD ESTATE, MUSEUM & GARDENS

In Vichy, France, Marjorie acquired pieces of the rare Orlov Service that Catherine the Great presented to Grigory Orlov after he led the successful coup that placed her on the Russian throne. Each piece is decorated with artillery banners in recognition of Orlov's military prowess. The amorous putti perhaps allude to their love affair.

LEFT: Vase with a painting of
The Herring Seller. St. Petersburg, 1853.
Imperial Porcelain Factory. Porcelain

ABOVE: Pieces from the Orlov Service.
St. Petersburg, 1762–65.
Imperial Porcelain Factory. Porcelain

Inspired by the colorful glass she had seen in the Soviet Union, Marjorie began to acquire Russian examples. Her collection grew to include pieces dating from the end of the seventeenth century to the eve of the Russian Revolution. To her extensive collection of imperial porcelain services she added banquet glasses, including numerous pieces from the Cottage Service. They were intended for use at the Alexandria Cottage in Peterhof, a small Gothic revival house Nicholas I built for his wife,

Pieces from the Cottage Service. Russia, ca. 1829. Imperial Glassworks. Glass, enamel, gilding

Alexandra Fedorovna, in the 1820s. Each piece bears the Cottage coat of arms—a blue shield with a small sword within a wreath of white roses—and the motto "For Faith, Tsar, and Fatherland."

Chandelier. Russia, ca. 1780. Glassworks of Prince Potemkin. Design attributed to Charles Cameron. Glass, gilt bronze

Marjorie Post with her Russian collection at Tregaron, early 1950s. Courtesy *Vogue* magazine

Now hanging in the breakfast room is one of the most remarkable pieces of Russian glass in the collection: a chandelier of green glass and gilt bronze. It was designed ca. 1780 by Charles Cameron, Catherine the Great's architect, for the Grand Ducal bedchamber at the Catherine Palace in Tsarskoe Selo.

When the Davies left the Soviet Union, they were sent to the American embassy in Brussels, but they did not stay long. They returned to Washington in 1939 at the outbreak of World War II. Back in the nation's capital, the Davies became central figures of the political and social scene. At the height of the Cold War, their Russian collection received special attention due to its unique size and scope.

ABOVE: *Twelve Monogram Egg*.
St. Petersburg, 1896. Firm of Carl Fabergé.
Mikhail Perkhin, workmaster.
Gold, champlevé enamel, diamonds

OPPOSITE: *Catherine the Great Easter Egg*.
St. Petersburg, 1914. Firm of Carl Fabergé.
Henrik Wigström, workmaster.
Gold, diamonds, pearls, enamel, silver, platinum, mirror

The nearly ninety objects by the Russian firm of Carl Fabergé today constitute a leading attraction at Hillwood, but Marjorie never considered them to be the most important part of her collection. She bought Fabergé most assiduously in the 1960s. With the possible exception of one piece—a small display case—she apparently did not acquire any Fabergé in the Soviet Union. The pink *Catherine the Great Easter Egg*, purchased in 1931 by her daughter Eleanor as a birthday present for Marjorie, was originally a gift from Nicholas II to his mother, Maria Fedorovna, in 1914. Its decoration reinterprets eighteenth-century French neoclassicism. Enamel areas *en camaieu* depict allegories of the arts and sciences after designs by François Boucher. Clusters of instruments rendered in various colors of gold, a technique revived from the eighteenth century, surround them. Also reminiscent of the Louis XVI era, Marjorie's preferred style, is the Yusupov music box, a gift from Princes Felix and Nicholas Yusupov to their parents on their twenty-fifth wedding anniversary in 1907. It features sepia enamel images of the various palaces owned by this wealthy aristocratic family.

Dating to 1896, the *Twelve Monogram Egg* was a gift from Tsar Nicholas to his mother after the death of his father, Alexander III. She was on vacation in France when she received it, along with a note from Nicholas.

You will by post be receiving a little parcel—it is from me. That silly man Fabergé came too late to send it by courier.... [March 22, 1896]

[The Empress replied from La Turbie] I can't find words to express to you, my dear Nicky, how touched and moved I was on receiving your ideal egg with the charming portraits of your dear, adored Papa. It is all such a beautiful idea, with our monograms above it all.... [March 28, 1896][6]

ABOVE: Candelabra. St. Petersburg, 1829. Designed by Ivan Ivanovich Gal'berg. Lapis lazuli, gilt bronze

RIGHT: *Portrait of Countess Samoilova*, by Karl Briullov. 1832–34. Oil on canvas

OPPOSITE: *A Boyar Wedding Feast*, by Konstantin Makovsky. 1883. Oil on canvas

It must have been awfully difficult to find the perfect birthday present for an inveterate collector like Marjorie. In 1967 her daughter Eleanor orchestrated the search in Paris for the ideal eightieth birthday gift for her mother. The pair of splendid lapis lazuli and gilt bronze candelabra that were once displayed in the private apartments of Tsarina Alexandra in the Winter Palace now flanks the mantelpiece in Hillwood's dining room.

Although Marjorie acquired Russian paintings sparingly, two superb canvases entered her collection in the later years. Karl Briullov's portrait of his close friend, Countess Julia Samoilova, is the most important example of the artist's work outside Russia. Depicted as she enters a room of her residence outside Milan, the beautiful countess wears a blue satin dress trimmed with lace. Her jewelry is fashioned in the latest archaeological revival style.

A Boyar Wedding Feast by Konstantin Makovsky still delights viewers as it did when it was painted in 1883. Makovsky romantically reinterprets a seventeenth-century wedding between two *boyar* families (members of the old Russian nobility). Two hundred years later, he carefully staged the composition and used costumes, silverware, and ivory objects from his own collection. The painting was exhibited in St. Petersburg, Moscow, and Paris before Makovsky sent it to the 1885 International Exposition in Antwerp.

APPAREL AND JEWELRY

From a turn-of-the-century Edwardian bride to a New York socialite to the *grande dame* of Washington and Palm Beach, Marjorie always presented herself with *savoir faire*. Her grace, charm, aesthetic taste, and sense of fashion earned her a place among the pantheon of iconic women of the twentieth century. Marjorie understood fashion and jewelry represented more than wealth and personal adornment. Today, Hillwood preserves over 175 of her garments and over 400 accessories, including shoes, hats, gloves, purses, and jewelry. As a result, it is a significant collection of twentieth-century personal apparel.

Charting her development from a Midwestern youth to a confident businesswoman, philanthropist, and collector, Marjorie's clothing tells her story through their rich fabrics, expert tailoring, and elegant designs. Her glamorous evening wear was created by early twentieth-century designers such as Lucille and Callot Soeurs. Russian-style day dresses that she wore in Moscow in 1937 and 1938 are now rare garments from the 1930s. Postwar fashions from the 1940s and 1950s include ensembles purchased at the high-end fashion houses of New York department stores Saks and Bergdorf Goodman. Of particular note is an evening dress created for the ceremony in which she received the French Legion of Honor in 1957.

LEFT: Presentation dress. Paris, 1929. Attributed to Callot Soeurs. Silk organza beading

OPPOSITE: Evening dress (detail). 1907–1908. Made by Callot Soeurs. Paris. Silk moiré, cotton moiré, silk crêpe

Marjorie acquired jewelry with the same passion she exercised in collecting her fine and decorative art. Interested in more than just wearing impressive jewels, she was a true connoisseur. Her collection ranges from designs by Cartier, Van Cleef and Arpels, and Harry Winston to such boutique designers as Verdura and George Headley in Kentucky.

Standing out among these is the emerald and diamond pendant brooch made by Cartier in the 1920s. This iconic piece, emblematic of the marriage of tradition and innovation for which the house of Cartier is known,

LEFT: Evening ensemble. New York, 1927–32. Made by Thurn. Silk crêpe (dress and cape), silk charmeuse, organza, lace (slip)

ABOVE: Day dresses. Italy, 1935–37. Designed by Rosie Renault. Wool, braided cotton cord, lamb's wool

OPPOSITE: Marjorie wore this dress to receive the French Legion of Honor in 1957. Evening dress. Italy, 1957. Designed by Eleanora Garnett. Silk velvet, taffeta faille

features more than 250 carats of carved Indian emeralds from the Mughal period. In the 1960s, Harry Winston created a turquoise and diamond necklace for Marjorie. She wore it paired with her Marie-Louis diadem (which she donated to the Smithsonian Institution) to the Red Cross Ball held in Palm Beach in 1967.

Historical pieces were an integral part of Marjorie's jewelry collection. One example is the vintage ruby and diamond parure that was reputedly made in the early nineteenth century for the Duchess of Oldenburg, a daughter of Grand Duchess Maria Nikolaevna and the granddaughter of Tsar Nicholas I.

Recognizing the important role jewelry plays in the world of artistic design, Marjorie purposely retained many of her pieces for the later enjoyment and education of the public. Her love and understanding of jewelry, much like her keen interest in porcelains and decorative art objects, have earned her the distinction of being both a major collector in her time and a twentieth-century icon of style.

[1] *There's a Reason* (Battle Creek, MI: Postum Company, n.d.).

[2] Ibid.

[3] Preparatory catalogue of the Post-Hutton collection, ca. 1927.

[4] Henriette Louise von Waldner Oberkirch, *Memoirs of Baroness d'Oberkirch, countess de Montbrison. Written by herself and ed. by her grandson, the Count de Montbrison*, vol. 3 (London: Colburn and Company, 1852), 60.

[5] Quoted in Richard Warrington Baldwin Lewis, *Edith Wharton: A Biography* (New York: Harper and Row, 1975), 374.

[6] Preben Ulstrup, "The House of Fabergé: The Imperial Family on Fabergé," *Treasures of Russia—Imperial Gifts* (Copenhagen: Royal Silver Room, 2002), 182–83.

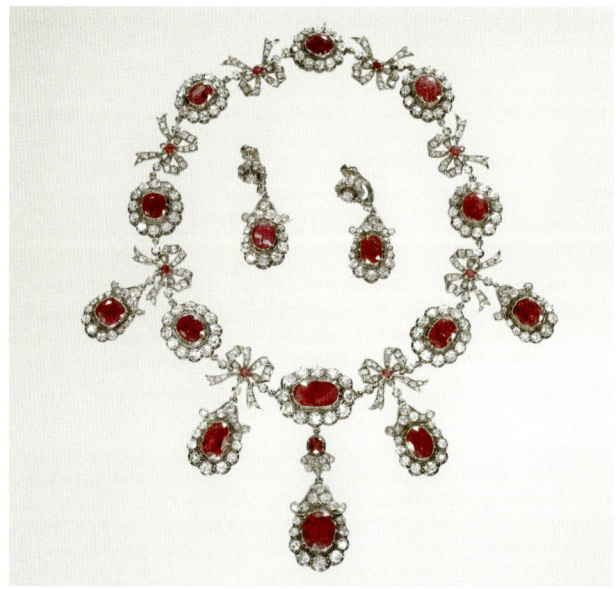

TOP: Necklace. United States, 1961. Designed by Harry Winston, Inc. Turquoise, diamonds, platinum

ABOVE: Necklace and earrings. Early 19th century. Rubies, diamonds, silver, gold

OPPOSITE: Pendant brooch. France, 1928. Designed by Cartier. Emeralds, diamonds, platinum, enamel

Gardens

Twenty-five acres of landscaped gardens and verdant natural woodlands reflect Old World luxury and echo the American country home tradition. Formal gardens extend from the mansion's terraces and porches in a series of "outdoor rooms" that complement the interior spaces and reflect Marjorie's love of color, intricate design, and association with European aristocracy.

PREVIOUS: View of the French parterre
OPPOSITE: Wisteria grows by the breakfast room
© Maxwell MacKenzie

A Country Estate in the Nation's Capital

In the murmuring of water flowing over stones, the crunch of gravel underfoot, and the brilliance of color blooming throughout the grounds, the sense of beauty and intention that characterized Marjorie Merriweather Post's way of life is experienced in each element of the garden oasis she created at Hillwood.

Marjorie built her first "Hillwood" in 1926 on the "Gold Coast" of Long Island, which is today best known as the setting for F. Scott Fitzgerald's 1925 novel *The Great Gatsby*. At that time, the American country estate tradition was thriving. Wealthy Americans sought to emulate the English landed gentry by building mansions on carefully landscaped properties as a way to provide welcome relief from crowded urban conditions. Marjorie's 125-acre property resembled the majestic country homes she had visited while traveling abroad with her father, C.W. Post. In the expanse of rolling lawn on Long Island she saw an opportunity to recreate the lifestyle of the English aristocracy she had come to admire.

When Marjorie was looking for a new home in Washington, D.C., in 1955, she discovered the twenty-five-acre estate called Arbremont. It echoed the American country home tradition—a trend that had come to an end due to the onset of income taxes—that she hoped to retain in the nation's capital. Captivated by the landscape, she decided to refurbish the neo-Georgian mansion with porches and terraces on all sides to provide easy access to the gardens, and she introduced new paths that connected the house to the garden walks and patios.

TOP: The first "Hillwood" on Long Island in the 1920s

ABOVE: Hillwood's main drive in the 1950s

OPPOSITE: View of the south portico across the Lunar Lawn
© Maxwell MacKenzie

Marjorie first hired the prominent landscape design firm of Umberto Innocenti and Richard Webel, of Long Island, to help her realize her vision for her new residence. A long winding entrance drive ran along terraced beds and ended at an enclosed motor court at the mansion's entrance. The French parterre was created to reflect Marjorie's interest in the culture of eighteenth-century France and extend the French emphasis of the adjacent French drawing room. Marjorie also hired the landscape architect Perry Wheeler, who designed the Lunar Lawn, motor court, and rose garden and further refined her plans for other features throughout the gardens.

Nearly thirty gardeners were employed to plant mature trees and shrubs that would create the visual effect of an established garden, one appropriate in age and scale to complement the grand house, landscape, and surrounding woodlands. During the spring and fall, when Marjorie lived at Hillwood, the gardens were filled with seasonal plants in an abundance of color. Flowering cherries, crabapples, magnolias, and dogwoods bloomed in concert with azalea, spirea, and rhododendron. Complementary beds were planted with spring bulbs, primroses, pansies, and forget-me-nots to provide a riot of color from April through June. In September, chrysanthemums filled the beds and borders to accentuate the blaze of colors from the trees in the gardens and woodlands. Today, the seasonal colors that Marjorie planned are extended through the summer with annual display beds, perennials such as geranium, hosta, and coral bells, and flowering shrubs of hydrangea, summersweet, and abelia. Winter shines with the bright berries of pyracantha, viburnum, and holly and the colorful bark of crape myrtle and shrub dogwood.

DRIVEWAY AND MOTOR COURT

Hillwood's winding driveway, designed by Innocenti and Webel, offers a vibrant welcome in the springtime and autumn. An elliptical motor court at the end of the drive formerly received vehicles and their passengers amid the abundant foliage of azaleas, dogwoods, and distinctive purple-leaf plum. In the center of the court stands a nineteenth-century stone sculpture of the Greek god Eros. Considered the most handsome of the immortals, this willowy god of love welcomes guests to Hillwood.

ABOVE: A sculpture of Eros in the motor court

LEFT: Hydrangeas add color to the summer gardens

OPPOSITE: Tropical plants and summer annuals around the Lunar Lawn

FRENCH PARTERRE

Petite archways lead into a world of European elegance and refinement. The French parterre—a formal garden with low, intricate plantings divided by footpaths and surrounded by walls of English ivy—evokes the feeling of a small formal garden in the eighteenth century.

Echoing the classical symmetry and geometry that typifies French garden design, the parterre is divided into four sections by gravel footpaths, channels of moving water, and a central pool lined with Italian glass tile. The carefully clipped boxwood hedges are planted in scroll patterns inspired by sixteenth-century ironwork. They recall decorative elements in the adjacent French drawing room and create a delightful design when seen from above. At one end of the parterre, Diana, goddess of the hunt, seems to dash from the woods with her hound; at the other end, marble sphinxes with winged cherubs on their backs adorn the terrace. Water flowing from each end along hand-carved limestone rills joins in the center pool and arches from the mouths of a playful seahorse and dolphin.

Marjorie installed a special bay window in her second floor bedroom suite so she could see the exquisite patterns of the formal French parterre while she wrote letters, answered phone calls, and held morning meetings with her staff. This "garden room" both extends the French design of the interiors and underscores Marjorie's obvious passion for the culture and luxury of eighteenth-century France.

OPPOSITE: French parterre in spring
© Maxwell MacKenzie

LEFT: Archways of the French parterre in fall

LEFT: Roses bloom throughout summer and into fall

OPPOSITE: A monument to Marjorie Merriweather Post in the rose garden
© Maxwell MacKenzie

ROSE GARDEN

In 1956 landscape architect Perry Wheeler, noted for assisting in the design of the White House Rose Garden, adapted a similar space to Marjorie's discerning taste. To complement the pergola, the stone steps leading to the putting green, and the garden's round shape, Perry emphasized the brickwork with his trademark intricate paving. At the center are four crown-shaped rose beds, each planted with a single cultivar of floribunda rose. Boxwood hedges echo the shape of the pergola to complete this circular "room."

Marjorie chose this tranquil garden as her final resting place. In November 1974, a little over a year after her death, her ashes were placed in the base of the granite monument at the center of the garden. An antique urn carved from rare deep purple porphyry rests above it. Seasonal flowers bloom around the monument—tulips in the spring, colorful annual flowers in the summer, and chrysanthemums in autumn. The base bears the Post coat of arms, with the engraved Latin phrase *In me mea spes omnis* (All my hopes rest in me), an apt motto for this generous, independent woman.

Flowers are laid at this site every year on March 15 in honor of Marjorie's birthday, a tradition begun by her longtime employee Gus Modig.

FRIENDSHIP WALK AND FOUR SEASONS OVERLOOK

In 1957 Marjorie's closest friends solved the age-old problem of what to give someone who has everything. They commissioned an English garden path that is affectionately called the Friendship Walk. A secret committee led by Frances Rosso, Lady Constance Lewis, and Sadie Pratt planned the Friendship Walk as a way to celebrate Marjorie's seventieth birthday and to honor her remarkable philanthropic contributions. Quite proud of the gift, Marjorie regularly showed the Friendship Walk to her guests.

Four statues representing the seasons stand at the entrance to the circular Four Seasons Overlook. A variety of trees, including magnolia, cherry, dogwood, crape myrtle, and witch hazel, offers colorful blooms throughout the year.

Friendship outstays the hurrying flight of years and aye abides through laughter and through tears.
—Tsarina Alexandra Fedorovna, the last empress of Russia

In the center, carved in black serpentine Italian marble, rests a plaque containing a quote about friendship from Tsarina Alexandra, the wife of Nicholas II. In creating the Four Seasons Overlook and the Friendship Walk, Marjorie's friends not only highlighted her love of gardens and nature, but they also seamlessly inserted her passion for imperial Russian culture. Inscribed names of the garden donors, who include ambassadors, congressmen, and other government officials, line the garden and emphasize the vast array of people who were influenced by the generosity and graciousness of Marjorie Merriweather Post.

Four Seasons Overlook
© Maxwell MacKenzie

LUNAR LAWN

Leo, a regal eighteenth-century stone lion, presides over an emerald expanse of more than thirteen thousand square feet of turf shaded by American elm trees and encircled by colorful seasonal plantings. Evergreen arborvitae and false cypresses, along with spring-blooming azaleas, camellias, dogwoods, and magnolias, enclose the space to create a grand outdoor room for entertaining.

From the south portico a glimpse of the Washington Monument rises above the treetops. Even though Hillwood exudes the feeling of a secluded country estate, it is less than four miles from the monument and the heart of Washington, D.C. The blue and white lawn chairs from the 1960s were Marjorie's way of combining modern trends with historic pieces. For her seventy-fifth birthday in 1962, her staff presented Marjorie with the flagpole across the lawn.

Marjorie hosted receptions on the Lunar Lawn for the political and social elite of Washington and for groups representing her philanthropic efforts, such as the Salvation Army, the National Symphony Orchestra, and veterans and soldiers returning from Vietnam. Today, celebrations held in conjunction with exhibition openings offer an air of contemporary elegance in the tradition of her unique sophisticated style.

ABOVE: Marjorie on the terrace with her dog Scampi, 1962

OPPOSITE: Lunar Lawn in fall

JAPANESE-STYLE GARDEN

A captivating hillside retreat enlivened with the sound of cascading water distinguishes Hillwood's Japanese-style garden. It was designed to imitate a traditional mountain setting in miniature, with a stream flowing through a series of pools and waterfalls, traversed by stone paths and bridges, and coming to rest in a tranquil pond.

Marjorie hired the notable Japanese garden designer Shogo Myaida to redesign an existing Asian garden. Myaida, who had been creating gardens on the East Coast since 1922, believed traditional Japanese gardens should be modified in the United States and be suited both to the specific property and to the personality of the owner. At Hillwood the result is a hybrid Japanese American garden that reflects Marjorie's aesthetic taste and her desire to display the variety of metal and stone Asian sculptures and statues she had collected over the years.

A pair of limestone satyrs greets visitors to several paths through the garden. Stepping stones cross the pool, and a stone walkway continues toward the bridges that connect the larger pond to a small island below. More than four hundred boulders create the appearance of a rocky mountainside embellished with traditional lanterns, bridges, and a stone pagoda. Although Myaida's plan originally called for few ornaments, Marjorie viewed the garden as an appropriate setting for displaying the treasures she had collected, including brass goldfish, phoenixes, cranes, and a figure of Hotei, the Japanese god of happiness and prosperity. In front of a small pool at the top of the garden sit two protective foo dogs.

OPPOSITE: The Japanese-style garden
© Maxwell MacKenzie

True to the harmonious fusion of Japanese and American elements, the garden flourishes with Japanese plants, such as Japanese pines, maples, azaleas, and false cypresses, as well as with Colorado blue spruces and other indigenous plants that grow in the adjacent woodlands.

A statue in the Japanese-style garden
© Maxwell MacKenzie

PUTTING GREEN

In the era of American country estates in the early to mid-twentieth century, recreational activities were integral design components of the landscape. At one time Hillwood boasted a swimming pool, tennis courts, a bridle path, stables, and dog kennels. A longtime proponent of living a healthy life, Marjorie emphasized exercise along with wholesome eating.

Surrounded by Japanese holly and snowball viburnum, the putting green is located down the rustic stone steps from the rose garden. The creeping bentgrass turf surface contains nine holes complete with cups and numbered pins. Vintage blue and white lawn furniture and wooden benches provide comfortable spots to relax. On cool evenings, Marjorie enjoyed bringing golf balls out to this putting green for a little entertaining competition with family and friends.

TOP AND LEFT: Snowball viburnums bloom around the putting green

OPPOSITE: Putting green

GREENHOUSES

In any season, the beauty and serenity of fragrant flowers can be found in the greenhouses at Hillwood. When Marjorie purchased the property, a small greenhouse existed on the grounds. She saw Hillwood as a perfect opportunity to support her growing collection of orchids—her favorite flower—and she invested in building four more greenhouses on the estate. She even hired an orchid curator to tend these temperamental beauties and to breed new varieties for her pleasure. Blooming orchids were always displayed in Marjorie's bedroom, the breakfast room, the first floor library, and the French drawing room. Large selections of orchids were often shipped from Hillwood to grace the rooms of her other estates.

Decades later, Hillwood still maintains the orchid collection to Marjorie's exacting standards, with more than two thousand specimens and hundreds of different varieties. In keeping with tradition, the mansion is enlivened with the exquisite colors and fragrance of these exotic flowers. Outside, visitors are encouraged to go into the greenhouses, where a staff member or volunteer takes care of these lovely orchids and other tropical plants. At Hillwood, one of the few public gardens in metropolitan Washington, current research and techniques are used to produce healthy plants and blooming flowers for arrangements the year round.

ABOVE: Greenhouse in fall

OPPOSITE: Exotic orchids thrive year-round in the greenhouse

CUTTING GARDEN

Row upon row of colorful blooms fill the beds of the cutting garden from late spring through fall. When she was in residence at Hillwood, Marjorie utilized this garden and other areas to provide a succession of seasonal blooms for arrangements throughout her home. The predominant types of flowers grown here have been used in arrangements since the 1950s and 1960s. Late spring and early summer bring bounties of lisianthus, snapdragon, larkspur, delphinium, and sweet William, while zinnia, celosia, and dahlia dominate in the summer and fall. Hillwood's floral designers often refer to photographs from the mid-twentieth century for inspiration on the style and placement of arrangements, sometimes putting a modern twist on Marjorie's traditional floral presentations.

PET CEMETERY

Limestone poodles, spaniels, and hounds with baskets of flowers adorn this secluded site, which is reached through quiet wooded paths. Planted with forget-me-nots, sweet box, and vinca groundcover, the pet cemetery is a tranquil memorial to the pet dogs Marjorie loved throughout her life. Scampi, her last dog, was laid to rest here in 1972. Many of Marjorie's family members shared her great love of dogs, and they continued to memorialize their beloved four-legged friends in the pet cemetery through the 1980s.

LEFT: Pet cemetery

OPPOSITE: Peony blooms in the cutting garden

DACHA

Set among the wooded paths of this classic American estate is a surprising Russian country house. Marjorie first encountered *dachas* during her months in the Soviet Union in the 1930s. She built a charming version of one at Hillwood to house a portion of her Russian collection. Constructed in 1969 during the Cold War, the dacha offers a nostalgic view of Russian culture. Some of the architectural elements, such as the whole-log construction and the intricate carvings, are authentic, while other details—the use of multiple bright colors and the onion-shaped domes on the roof—are American adaptations of motifs that are typically found on Russian churches but not on rustic homes.

The dacha originally housed a collection of Russian decorative arts from the nineteenth and early twentieth centuries. Madame Frances Rosso, the American wife of the Italian ambassador to the Soviet Union in the 1930s, gave the objects to Marjorie in the 1960s.

Today, this unexpected emblem of Russian culture amidst the grounds of a great American estate stands as a reminder of the role Marjorie Merriweather Post played as cultural ambassador. Democratic and American to the core, Marjorie left Hillwood as a gift to the nation, and with it her valuable collection and lasting appreciation for the decorative arts of eighteenth-and nineteenth-century Europe and Russia.

Dacha
© Maxwell MacKenzie

SELECTED RESOURCES

Chung, Estella. *Living Artfully: At Home with Marjorie Merriweather Post*. Washington, D.C.: Hillwood Museum and Gardens Foundation, in association with D Giles Limited, London, 2013.

Fisher, Frederick J. "Marjorie Merriweather Post." *Antiques*, March 2003, 82–87.

Hillwood Museum and Gardens. Washington, D.C.: Hillwood Museum and Gardens Foundation, 2000.

Odom, Anne, and Liana Paredes Arend. *A Taste for Splendor: Russian Imperial and European Treasures from the Hillwood Museum*. Alexandria, VA: Art Services International, 1998.

Paredes, Liana. "Furnishing Hillwood: Marjorie Merriweather Post's Passion for French Style." *Antiques*, March 2003, 88–95.

Rubin, Nancy. *American Empress: The Life and Times of Marjorie Merriweather Post*. 2nd ed. Lincoln, NE: iUniverse Star, 2004. First published 1995 by Villard Press.

Copyright © 2015 Hillwood Estate, Museum & Gardens
All rights reserved.

Published by
Hillwood Estate, Museum & Gardens
4155 Linnean Avenue, NW
Washington, DC 20008

No part of the contents of this book may be reproduced, stored in a retrieval system, or transmitted in any form or by any means, electronic, mechanical, photocopying, recording, or otherwise, without the written permission of Hillwood Estate, Museum & Gardens.

General Editor: Lynn Rossotti
Publication Coordinator: Amy Pastan
Editor: Nancy Eickel
Design: Skelton Design

Printed in China through Asia Pacific Offset

Cataloging-in-Publication Data is available from the Library of Congress
ISBN Hardcover: 978-1-931485-11-1
ISBN Softcover: 978-1-931485-12-8

ADDITIONAL IMAGE CREDITS

RENÉE COMET: p. 81, p. 82 (left)

JOHN DEAN: p. 31, p. 38 (above), p. 43 (top and above), p. 45 (below), p. 47, p. 49 (top), p. 50 (left), P.105 (top)

ALEX JAMISON: p. 33, p. 44

JESSIE MARCOTTE: pp. 86-87, p. 95, p. 101

EDWARD OWEN: p. 39 (right), p. 41 (top and left), p. 45 (top), p. 46 (left), pp. 52-53, p. 55, p. 56, p. 58 (left and below), p. 59, p. 60 (above, top left, and top right), p. 61, p. 62 (above and right), p. 63, p. 64 (left and above), p. 65, p. 66 (above and right), p. 67, p. 68, p. 70 (left and above), p. 71 (left and above), p. 72 (left and right), p. 73 (left and above), p. 74, p. 75 (left), p. 76, p. 77, p. 78 (above and right), p. 79, p. 80, p. 82 (above), p. 83, p. 84 (top and above), p. 85, back cover

TONY POWELL: p. 49 (right), p. 50 (above)

FRONT COVER: Ivy covers the mansion exterior in the French parterre. © Maxwell MacKenzie

FRONT FLAP (softcover): Garden sculpture. © Maxwell MacKenzie

FRONT ENDPAPER (hardcover): Swan fountain in the French parterre

FRONTISPIECE (hardcover): Garden sculpture. © Maxwell MacKenzie

CONTENTS: Portrait of Marjorie Merriweather Post, ca. mid-1930s

BACK ENDPAPER (hardcover): Flowering shrubs line a garden walkway. © Maxwell MacKenzie

BACK FLAP (softcover) and OPPOSITE: Portrait of Marjorie Merriweather Post. By Frank O. Salisbury. England, ca.1930. Oil on canvas

BACK COVER: Dining room table (detail)